Happy Reading!
Brooklynn

Bailey Cannon

The Day After Spring Break

Written by: Aimee Lary & Bailey Cannon
Illustrated by Adua Hernandez

First Edition

Hardback:ISBN 978-1-7365623-1-4

Paperback Cover ISBN 978-1-7365623-0-7

To our angels in Heaven who watch over us daily: "Great Grandmother" Jeweline Calloway, "Papa" Arthur White and "Uncle Uncle" Keenan Zeno, because even in your absence you inspire us.

I was enjoying a normal spring break filled with fun, family, and friends in 3rd grade when everything changed.

Towards the end of the week, there was a lot of talk on the news about the Coronavirus. It seemed kind of important, but I had no idea what they were talking about. Was it a new dance? A popular drink? A game? Or maybe some type of animal? I had no clue! I overheard my family talking about it; they seemed anxious and concerned.

The next day, I woke up to find out that my school district was closing for a few days. Later that week, the news said that my school — and many others — would be closing for the rest of the school year. What a shocker! This wasn't just happening in my school district, but all over the whole wide world! Well, maybe not in Antarctica; it's probably too cold for the Coronavirus to survive there.

At first, I was really excited – NO SCHOOL!?
This is the best news ever!

Then I thought about it: no school meant that I may never see my teachers again. It meant, no more talking to my friends during lunch or playing with them at recess. It meant no free time in the gym or swapping LOL dolls after school. My feelings of excitement about not going to school quickly changed - now I felt confused, sad, and upset.

I had to know more. What was this Coronavirus? Why does my school have to close? I learned that it was a dangerous virus that affects the respiratory system. In other words, it makes your lungs weak, which makes it difficult for you to breathe. Mom said that some other symptoms are coughing and high fever. She taught me the importance of washing my hands, staying 6 feet apart, and wearing a mask over my mouth and nose.

Have you ever heard of Mr. Clean? The man with no hair on the cleaning commercials? Well my Mom became Ms. Clean! She cleaned doorknobs, light switches, lamps, tables, chairs, couches, kitchen, bedrooms, bathrooms, and even the garage. If I touched anything, she would remind me to wash my hands and use sanitizer. At one point, I started wearing gloves because she was driving me crazy! And, she wasn't the only thing driving me crazy.

One day, Mom told me that I would be going to school virtually. Virtually?! What does that mean? Basically, I would be doing my schoolwork from home using the internet. This is how I received my first introduction to Zoom – a video conferencing tool that lets you use a web camera to meet with others.

My day would begin and end with Zoom; everybody was doing it. During online school, I had Zoom meetings, classwork, and a ton of homework to do. Two assignments in Reading, two assignments in Writing, two assignments in Math, and two assignments in Science and Social Studies. Do you know how many assignments that is a day? Ten! It was overwhelming, and that drove me crazy.

Besides being tired from all the schoolwork, the virtual school experience was pretty cool. I enjoyed playing games like charades, who am I, and participating in show and tell with my teacher and classmates.

My favorite part about virtual school was being able to work with my Mom and Dad. If I didn't understand something being taught, my parents were there to help me. They also encouraged me in those times when I felt like giving up because I was frustrated; I even think they got a little frustrated sometimes too.

At this point in May, I can't believe everything has been shut down since March. Mom says that its only been a month and a half, but it feels like an eternity. I have not been out of the house besides going to the park for long walks with Mom.

There was nothing open but grocery stores and gas stations. Then, finally, things began to change, and buildings began to reopen. Places like restaurants, clothing stores, hair salons, banks, and my favorite, the trampoline park...

Businesses are open, but they look different, in a safer kind of way. There are markings on the floor to remind people to stay 6 feet apart and which direction to walk down the aisle. Someone stays at the front of the store to keep a tally of how many people are coming in and out. There are hand sanitizing stations all over the place, as well as signs to remind people to wear a mask — just like Mom always says.

I used to think that only doctors and nurses wore masks, but now cashiers, mail carriers, grocery clerks, and even teachers all wear masks.

Even though my mask has a really cool design, I don't like wearing it all the time. It makes my face hot and sweaty and sometimes it's hard for me to breathe.

My Mom talks about the, "bright light at the end of the tunnel." To me, this means that good things happen during bad times. She reminds me that the mask keeps me, our family, the community, and the world safe – even if some people don't agree.

There are times when I ask why the Coronavirus is happening? And when will all of this be over? Remember, you're not alone. Just look around, we're all in this together. And because of that, we're stronger!

So let's keep doing our part by wearing our mask, washing and sanitizing our hands. Don't wait for your Mom, Dad or Teacher to tell you to do it. Do it because you want to keep everyone safe. Do it because it's the right thing to do.

Who knew that everything in my life would change
the day after spring break.

About the Authors

Aimee Lary and Bailey Cannon are a fun-loving dynamic mother-daughter duo who hail from the Lone Star State. Aimee graduated from Prairie View A&M University with a Bachelor of Arts in Communications and a Master of Arts in Counseling. For the past 8 years, she has served as an educator in both the elementary and secondary levels and Bailey is currently an ambitious 4th grader with a passion for dance. The pandemic has given them the space to reconnect with their love for children's literacy. In addition to children's books, they both enjoy spending time with family, cooking together, and playing putt-putt golf. They want to share their belief with the world that there is an author in all of us because everyone has a story to tell.